STRANGE
OLD SCOTS
CUSTOMS
AND
SUPERSTITIONS

Lang**Syne**

PUBLISHING

WRITING *to* REMEMBER

Lang**Syne**

PUBLISHING

WRITING *to* REMEMBER

79 Main Street, Newtongrange,
Midlothian EH22 4NA
Tel: 0131 344 0414 Fax: 0845 075 6085
E-mail: info@lang-syne.co.uk
www.langsyneshop.co.uk

Printed by Blissetts
© Lang Syne Publishers Ltd 2019

ISBN 9-780946-264-056

INTRODUCTION

The Scots have always been a superstitious race. Our Pictish ancestors were simple savages who painted their faces, believed in black magic and worshipped the sun. A selected number were burned alive each year as sacrifices.

Down through the centuries many other unusual practices became a normal part of life as the numbers of this, and other tribes, multiplied.

Weddings couldn't be held on certain days . . . precautions were taken to ensure that evil spirits didn't steal the souls of the dying . . . and so on.

Remarkably some of these ancient customs still survive today but others have passed into history. And it is possibly no bad thing — as you may agree after reading this book — that a lot of the old beliefs have been swept away for ever.

John Mackay's illustrations are spread throughout this volume. On the front cover he gives his impressions of an old Scots wedding. All the costumes are taken from David Allan's painting in the National Gallery of Scotland of "A Highland Wedding at Blair Atholl in 1780." The bridegroom's sporran and breeches are also authentic. The fiddler is the famous Neil Gow.

The Back cover shows children out guising at Hallowe'en.

Adapted from "Old Scottish Customs — Local and General" by E.J.Guthrie, published in 1885.
Original illustrations by John Mackay.

Trial marriages for a year and a day

Prior to the Reformation in the sixteenth century, when Scotland was a Catholic country rather than a Protestant one, trial marriages were very common.

At annual fairs the unmarried of both sexes would choose a companion with whom to live for a year and a day. This custom was known as handfasting, or hand-in-fist.

If the parties remained pleased with each other at the expiry of the term of probation, they remained together for life; if not, they separated, and were free to find another partner.

Priests were sent out from the various monasteries into the surrounding districts to look after all hand-fasted persons, and bestow the nuptial benediction on those willing to receive it.

If either of the parties insisted on a separation, and a child was born during the year of trial, it was to be taken care of by the father only and ranked among his lawful children next after his heirs. The offspring was not treated as illegitimate, because the custom was justified as making way for a peaceful and happy marriage.

Tradition tells that a desperate feud broke out between the clans of Macdonald of Sleat, and Macleod of Dunvegan, on the Isle of Skye, after one particular trial marriage hit the rocks. A Macdonald chief decided he didn't want to marry his Macleod lady which brought the retort from the Chief of Macleod: "If there is to be no wedding bonfire then there will be one to solemnize the divorce!"

Accordingly, he burned and laid waste the lands of the Macdonalds. They retaliated with a vengeance and for months afterwards there was much spilling of blood and wrecking of homes.

Hand-fasting was considered to be socially unacceptable by the Reformers and they strove by every means to repress it. In 1562, the Kirk-Session of Aberdeen decreed that all hand-fasted persons should be married. With the exception of the Highland districts, the time-honoured practice of living together for "a year and a day" ceased to exist shortly after the Reformation.

Handfasting could end in tragedy — as in this feud between the MacLeods and Macdonalds.

Ale, whisky and brandy — just to arrange wedding!

Making wedding arrangements at the tavern.

When a young man set his heart on matrimony he didn't go to see his sweetheart's parents but adjourned to the tavern instead! There he told the landlady of his intentions and she then sent for the girl who was the object of his affections.

The maiden thus honoured seldom failed to appear; and the marriage was arranged over constant supplies of ale, whisky, and brandy.

The common form of betrothal on such occasions was as follows: the parties linked the thumbs of their right hands, which they pressed together, and vowed fidelity.

"My sweetest May, let love incline ye,
Accept a heart which he designs ye;
And as you cannot, love, regret it,
Syne for its faithfulness receive it.
'Tis proof as shot to birth or money,
But yields to what is sweet and bonny.
Receive it then, wi' a kiss and a smiley,
There's my thumb, it will ne'er beguile ye."

On the second day after their wedding, an event known as the creeling took place.

The newly married couple and their friends assembled in a field and a basket was filled with stones. The young men took turns carrying this and allowed themselves to be caught and kissed by the maidens who accompanied them.

At length the young husband was given the task of carrying the basket but tradition stipulated that he had to carry it for much longer than the others.

None of the other young women were permitted to take pity and relieve him of the burden, but at length his new life partner would come to the rescue.

The basket went round again, more fun ensued, then the entire company dined together and talked over the events of the day.

This custom, popular in the Borders and some parts of Ayrshire, was believed to mirror the cares which a man incurred in marrying, but of which it was in the power of a good wife to relieve him.

Silver spoons for the bride and groom!

In olden times it was customary for Scots couples contemplating marriage to pay a visit to Parliament Close, Edinburgh.

This was the home of the capital's silversmiths where the bride and groom would select their silver spoons . . . then just as important a part of any marriage as the ring, cake and bridesmaids.

Usually two journeys were made involving the silver spoons. The first, a few weeks before the ceremony, to select the spoons and give details of the initials to be marked on them; the other to receive and pay for the spoons.

Throw a sixpence to stop a marriage

"Giving Up the Names" was the title of a ceremony in which the names of couples intending marriage were announced during church services. Anyone who wished to stop a marriage taking place could throw down a sixpence and state their reasons for objecting. This, however, was seldom done.

Tuesdays and Thursdays were the most popular days for marriages in Galloway. One prominent minister in the area recorded that of 450 marriages he conducted all but seven took place on these days.

Rough justice for wayward spouses

It is natural to assume that in the old lawless times every sort of immorality would've been condoned or at least overlooked. But it was not so.

A man could steal a sheep from a flock passing through the village and be praised for his dexterity. He might slay a rival in fair combat and be hailed as a hero. He might elope with the girl of his dreams even though her parents objected and be admired for his courage; but dallying with his neighbour's wife was altogether another matter.

Punishment for such gross misconduct included having to run the gauntlet. At a stated time villagers assembled in the transgressor's house. They stripped him to his shirt and tied him to the back of a pony cart. His bundle of clothes was thrown into the back and he was forced to march or run through the streets followed by a hooting, jeering crowd.

At the head of the village his hands were cut free and his clothes thrown at him, a signal that he was now free to return home.

If the culprit was a wife her case was brought before a jury of matrons who considered all the evidence. If found guilty the accused woman was subjected to the humiliating ordeal of riding the stang.

This was a long pole carried by a party of men. She was taken through the streets and then, without any dignity, tumbled into the nearest stretch of water!

Unfaithful wife is tossed into the water.

Shame of the Sunday Sprees

Sunday Sprees were once the shame of Scotland.

Sabbath after Sabbath bands of disorderly men met at an appointed place and drank to great excess.

The proceedings began early in the morning — indeed they were usually the continuation of Saturday night's spree — and were not brought to a close until late on Sunday evening. It was also said that while the men did their drinking in the open air, the wives had their spreed within doors so that Sabbath desecration was the rule with both sexes.

Rowan tree and Red thread

A popular charm, to guard against the evils of witchcraft, was a small piece of the branch of the rowan tree wrapped round with red thread and sewn into clothes.

"Rowan tree and red thread
Will drive the witches a' wud."

Fed-up husbands in Langholm used to have the perfect solution for nagging wives — an iron instrument called the 'Branks'. It fitted onto a woman's head and projected a sharp spike into her mouth which held the tongue firmly in position.

Wives who went too far were often paraded through the town wearing the Branks and besides the obvious discomfort also had to endure the laughing taunts of their neighbours.

It is said that the shock of it all never failed to transform a woman into an obedient spouse, and as a local historian observed: "The Branks was much to be preferred to the ducking stool, which not only endangered the health of the patient, but gave the tongue liberty between each dip."

Punishment for a wayward wife at Langholm.

Guard cattle against evil!

When a cow was taken suddenly ill in Shetland the cause was usually put down to elf-shot . . . a type of spirit called Trows, said to be different in their nature from fairies, had fired a stone arrow and wounded the animal with it.

There were never any visible signs of a wound but certain folk claimed they could trace it by feeling the flesh in a certain way. A cure was effected by repeating particular words over the cow.

They also folded a cinder in a leaf taken from a particular part of the psalm-book, and secured it in the hair of the cow. This was not only considered an infallible cure, but was believed to serve as a charm against future attacks.

On many Scots farms, when a calf was born, a cat was set on its neck, drawn along its back, and then seated on the cow's back. Next it was drawn down one side of the mother and pulled up the other, tail foremost.

This ceremony was supposed to prevent the cow being carried away by trows while in a weak state and was styled "enclosing the cow in a magic circle."

The trows were said to have enormous appetites when it came to eating and drinking. So theft to provide food was the usual reason given for them plundering cattle.

Folk who caught a glimpse of the inside of a trow's dwelling claimed they had seen their own animal led to be slaughtered while, at the same time, their friends on the surface of the earth saw her fall by an invisible hand and tumble over a precipice.

Sometimes, also, the trows required a nurse for their children, they also having a time to be born and a time to die. Therefore females engaged in nursing their own children had to be watched very carefully in case they were carried off to perform the office of wet nurse to a little trow who had either lost its mother, or whose station amongst her own race exempted her from the drudgery of nursing her offspring.

Never ignore
Fiery Cross!

When a chieftain wished to summon members of his clan in an emergency he killed a goat. Next he made a cross of light wood, burned its extremities in the fire, then extinguished the flames in the animals's blood.

This was called the Fiery Cross, also *Creau Toigh,* or the Cross of Shame, because disobedience to what the symbol implied incurred infamy.

The cross was transferred from hand to hand, and sped through the chief's territories with incredible speed. At sight of every man, from 16 to 60, was obliged to go to the appointed meeting place.

Anyone who ignored the summons exposed himself to the penalties of fire and sword "which were emblematically denoted by the bloody and burned marks, upon the fiery herald of woe."

Summons of the Fiery Cross!

Crusading tale of the Blue Blanket

The Blue Banner was once the most powerful flag in all Scotland. It was the ancient symbol of the trades of Edinburgh and on its appearance every tradesman in the country was obliged to drop whatever they were doing and obey the commands of the Convener who took charge of the Banner.

According to an old tradition, this standard was flown in the Holy Wars by a band of crusading Edinburgh citizens and was first planted on the walls of Jerusalem when that city was stormed by the Christian army under the famous Godfrey de Bouillon.

James III, after being kept prisoner for nine months in Edinburgh Castle by his rebellious nobles, was freed by the citizens of Edinburgh who raised the Blue Blanket, assaulted the Castle and took it by surprise.

In gratitude James presented them with another banner — a blue silken pennon, with powers to display it in defence of their King, country, and their own rights, when these were assailed.

Burning the chaff

Throughout Scotland it was once the custom for the relatives of the dead — the day after the funeral — to carry the chaff and bed-straw on which the person had died, to some hillock in the neighbourhood of the house where it was then burned.

As to the funeral itself, a time was never allocated. Ten in the morning was understood to be the time of assembling, and two or three in the afternoon as that of the "lifting."

The intervening hours were spent in prayers, graces, eating and drinking. A look-out kept position from a vantage point and once it was clear that no further mourners were approaching the signal was given for the procession to the churchyard.

These were the order of services in the course of the day:—

1st Service — bread and cheese with ale and porter.

2nd Service — Glass of rum with "burial bread."

3rd Service — Pipes filled with tobacco. Women who sat at the late-wake were given the duty of preparing the pipes.

4th Service — Glass of port wine with cake.

5th Service — Glass of sherry with cake.

6th Service — Glass of whisky.

7th Service — Glass of wine not specified.

8th Service — Thanks returned for the whole.

Then the whole order of service began all over again as another individual made his appearance.

In the Campsie district everyone from the surrounding area was invited to the funeral. The mourners were served, seated on boards in the barn, with ale, whisky, then shortbread, followed by liquor and a piece of currant bread. Later a third supply of either whisky or wine was served. After this came bread and cheese, pipes and tobacco.

This feast was called a service; sometimes it was repeated, in which case it was called a double service.

No matter the distance from the place of interment, it was customary for the attendants to carry the coffin on hand-spokes.

A special messenger went round inviting people to the funeral. No written invitations were issued and although the normal arrival time was 10 a.m. the burial never took place until the evening.

It was customary to have two Lykewakes, when the young friends and neighbours watched the corpse. These were merry or sorrowful according to the position or rank of the deceased.

Arriving at the funeral

Ringing bells to chase away evil spirits

After death it is still customary in some Highland districts to place a bowl of salt and a bowl of earth in the coffin of a dead person. The latter represents the "corruptible body" while the former marks the "immortal spirit."

In days gone by when a local worthy was dying the church bells were rung so that everyone could go to the house and wish the soul farewell. As soon as the last breath had been drawn windows and doors were thrown open to ensure that the spirit of their dear departed would have an uninterrupted road to whatever destination the Lord had provided.

The ringing bells also had the effect of warding off evil spirits which lay in wait to steal souls.

Transition to the world of spirits

The Magistrates and Kirk Session of Montrose used to meet once a year to give out badges to folk forced to beg to be sure of a crust.

When a person lay on his or her deathbed it was customary for all friends and relations to gather round.

Everyone united in solemn worship singing a psalm, such as the 23rd, in low and solemn melody. This ensured a proper transition of the dying person's soul into the spirit world.

Rise up gude wife! —
Childrens' old Hogmanay song

Rise up! gude wife and shak' yer feathers!

At Hallowe'en and Hogmanay kids, especially in country districts, transform themselves into "Guisers" or "Guizards" by blacking their faces and putting on fancy dress.

Then they tour the homes of neighbours doing amusing turns in return for money and food.

An old rhyme, which used to be recited by groups of children on the doorstep, goes as follows:

Rise up! guid wife, and shak' yer feathers,
And dinna think that we are beggars,
We are bairns come out to play,
Rise up! and gie's oor Hogmanay.

The day will come when ye'll be deid,
Ye'll neither care for meal nor breid,
Rise up! guid wife and dinna spare,
Ye'll hae less, we'll hae mair.

Up stocks, doon stools!
Dinna think that we are fules,
We are bairns come out to play,
Rise up! and gie's us oor Hogmanay.

Marry in May and yer bairns will decay

Our forefathers believed that a bride would have bad luck if she met a priest, a monk or a hare on the way to church, and good luck if a spider, toad, cat or wolf crossed her path.

Horse shoes, once kept on barn doors to ward off evil spirits, are still given to young couples, but the fear of marrying during the month of May is no longer with us.

Mothers used to warn their off-spring: "Marry in May and yer bairns will decay."

Giant football game

Once a year the married men challenged the bachelors to a robust game of football at Coldingham, the Berwickshire seaside village.

The shore formed a boundary for the married men; that of the unmarried men was more difficult to get at, being a hole in the earth about a mile and a half west from the town.

Waddin bawes, Waddin braws!

Weddings used to last a week but as time passed they became more tame affairs. This led older women, recalling the glorious occasions of yesteryear, to remark that the "spirit o' waddings has left the country."

"Waddin bawes" was the term used to describe money tossed amongst the people at marriages. "Waddin braws" was the description given to wedding dresses.

"Waddin sarks" was the marvellous name given to the practice by which the bride made a shirt for her new husband before the wedding, thus demonstrating her skills in the craft of needlework.

A country lad once remarked to his friend that he "never intended to take Maggie (his wife), but the cutty saw this, flew to his neck, and measured him for the sark, and so I was obliged to have her."

Robin Hood's Scots games are banned!

The Robin Hood Games were once an important event on the calendar of many Scots towns and cities, particularly Edinburgh.

Some of the events held as part of this festival poked fun at the pomp and circumstance of church and state.

A noted historical work, the Domestic Annals of Scotland, describes what took place at these whimsical merry-makings:—

"At the approach of May, the people assembled and chose some respectable individuals of their number — very grave and reverend citizens perhaps — to act the parts of Robin Hood and Little John, of the Lord of Disobedience or the Abbot of Unreason, and make sports and jocosities of them.

"If the chosen actors felt it was inconsistent with their tastes, gravity, or engagements, to don a fantastic dress, caper and dance and incite their neighbours to do the like, they would only be excused on paying a fine.

"On the appointed day, always a Sunday or holiday, the people assembled in their best attire and in military array, and marched in blythe procession to some neighbouring field, where the fitting preparations had been made for their amusement.

"Robin Hood and Little John robbed bishops, fought with pinners, and contended in archery amongst themselves as they had done in reality two centuries before. The Abbot of Unreason kicked up his heels and played antics like a modern pantaloon. Maid Marian also appeared upon the scene in flower-spirit kirtle, and with bow and arrows in hand, and doubtless slew hearts as she had formerly done.

"Mingling with the mad scene were the Morris-dancers, with their fantastic dresses and jingling bells.

"And so it continued till the Reformation, when a sudden stop was put to the whole affair by severe penalties imposed by Act of Parliament."

Breaking eggs of unpopular birds

The curious game of Blinchamp was once very popular as a favourite way of getting rid of the eggs of unpopular birds like the Corbie or Hoodiecrow.

When a nest was found belonging to one of these birds the eggs were taken out and laid out in rows a little apart from one another.

The first player was then blindfolded and given a stick. He would then walk forward trying to break as many eggs in one swoop as possible.

The one who broke the most eggs at the end of the contest was declared winner, or blinchamp — hence the name of the game.

Finding the cure at Strathnaver

A well at Strathnaver in Sutherland was credited with curing all sorts of ailments. Folk walked into the water backwards, took their dip, and left a small coin as a token of their appreciation for any help which might be given.

After this, and without looking back, they had to walk straight out of the loch on to dry land and continue to go as far away as possible from the water's edge without turning round.

Why right hand was not baptised

When children were baptised in the Borders it was customary to leave the right hand of male children unbaptised. This ensured that they would not desist from inflicting powerful blows on their enemies in the event of any dispute.

Death in the turn of a dish

St Andrew's Well on the Island of Lewis was frequently consulted as an oracle when anyone was dangerously ill. A wooden tub full of this water was brought to the sick man's room and a small dish was set floating on the surface of the water: if it turned sunwise it was supposed the patient would recover, otherwise he must die.

Cockenzie's evil omen

In the East Lothian fishing village of Cockenzie a fisher refused to go to sea if a pig or a lame man crosed his path on the way to the beach,

Cauld iron!

Cry on fishing boat to ward off bad luck.

Also, if a stranger met him and was first to issue the greeting "gude mornin", the seafarer took this as an evil omen, and stayed home for at least all of that day.

It was regarded as extreme bad luck to take the Lord's name in vain while at sea. If this happened one of the crew would call out "cauld airn" and, to counteract the evil that such a blasphemy was sure to incur, everyone had to grab hold of the first piece of iron which came within his reach, and hold it for a time between his hands. This counteracted ill-luck which otherwise would've followed the boat for the rest of the day.

How demon's curse became a blessing

The remedial qualities of certain wells were well-known to the ancients. Roman and Greek physicians were great believers in the curing powers of water brought up from deep below ground.

Our Pictish ancestors in Scotland believed that wells were originally made by demons for the destruction of mankind but that the Saints had intervened to transform this curse to a blessing.

Many folk actually worshipped wells but this "heathenish" activity was discouraged after the Reformation.

St Fillan's Well was, like some others, long believed to cure insanity. Luckless sufferers were thrown from a high rock down into the well, and then locked up for the night in the ruined chapel.

Some 200 patients were taken there every year and after a bath in the well and other ceremonies the patient was tied to an ancient pillar. If he or she were found loose in the morning, the cure was deemed to have been effective.

Country women used to take their weak and delicate children to St Fillan's. They bathed them in the water and left some pieces of cloth hanging on the neighbouring bushes as a present or offering to *Cella Fillan,* the tutelar saint of the parish.

This stopped in the middle of the 18th century when, at the minister's command, the well was filled up with stones.

It was said that from time immemorial three stones have been perpetually whirling round and round a well on the shores of Loch Torridon.

Touch the steeple and you're a free man!

To be found guilty of a serious crime and sentenced to death by the court in Dingwall was not always the absolute end. For if the prisoner could make his escape, get past a crowd before anyone could lay a finger on him, and touch the church steeple, he was a free man.

Supplying free milk to spare brownie's rod

Some time ago natives of the Western Isles believed in the existence of the *gruagach*, a female spectre of the class of brownies to whom the dairymaids made frequent libations of milk.

The *gruagach* was said to be an innocent being who frolicked or gambolled among the pens and folds. She was armed solely with a pliable rod, with which she beat any who annoyed her.

As late as 1770 dairymaids were in the habit of placing a quantity of milk on a hollow stone for the *gruagach*. If they neglected this duty they were sure to feel the weight of the brownie's rod the following day.

Claret galore!

Rory More's Horn at Dunvegan Castle on the Isle of Skye must have been viewed with mixed feelings by the young lairds of MacLeod.

For, to prove their manhood on coming of age, the MacLeods had to drain its entire contents of one and a half pints of claret . . . in one continuous go!

Special powers of the May Dew

Early on the morning of the first of May young people would go in groups to the fields to gather May Dew which they patted over their faces. This was said to promise physical and mental well-being for the year ahead.

Fair maidens might be seen tripping through the meadows

before sun·rise, having been told by their elders "that if they got up in time to wash their faces with dew before the sun appeared they would have fine complexions for the remainder of the year."

To this day the custom is still popular in some parts of Scotland, particularly Edinburgh where the summit of Arthur's Seat is always a popular destination for many folk just before dawn on the first day of May.

Shooting for silver arrows

The ancient and once royal sport of archery was greatly encouraged in Scotland by King James I. During his reign all boys had to take lessons at the age of 12 and prove themselves competent with bow and arrow.

Each year competitions were held with silver arrows presented by the King to the royal burghs and the winners were given silver medals which they could affix to these as testimony of their skills.

There were two kinds of archery — pointblank archery or shooting at 'butts', and popinjay archery.

The popinjay is a bird known in heraldry. It was cut out of wood, fixed at the end of a pole, and placed at a distance of 120 feet on the steeple of the Abbey.

The archer who brought down the mark was honoured with the title of Captain of the Popinjay, and received a parti-coloured sash. In archery clubs, such as Kilwinning in Ayrshire, he was master of all ceremonies for the ensuing year. He sent invitation cards to the ladies, gave them a splendid ball, and transmitted his honours by a medal with suitable devices affixed to a silver arrow.

Bread and cheese for souls of the slain

Until the middle of the last century it was a custom for people to visit the Chapel of St Tears, Wick, on Innocent's Day. The Chapel was dedicated to the Holy Innocents and bread and cheese was left as an offering to the souls of the children slain by Herod.

People used to come from all over Caithness to a holy loch at Dunnet which was credited with healing powers. They cast a penny into the water and then walked, or were carried round the loch.

When they recovered their cure was ascribed to the mystic virtues of the Halie Loch; and if they didn't, their lack of faith was blamed.

Why Robert the Bruce gave help to lepers

King Robert the Bruce was seriously ill with all the symptoms of leprosy when he drank water from a medicinal spring near Ayr. As a result he began to recover, and in gratitude founded the priory of Dominican Monks. They were charged with praying daily for his continued good health. After Robert's death those masses were continued for the salvation of his soul.

He had also ordered the construction of eight houses around the well for the accommodation of lepers, who were each allowed eight bolls of oat-meal and 28 shillings Scots money per annum.

The site of the houses became known as King's Ease. Robert presented a drinking horn to each leprous person and this continued to be hereditary in the house to which it was first granted.

Robert the Bruce's house for lepers at Ayr.

First horse races

King James IV established horse racing as a royal sport and the first notice of horse racing in Britain occurred in his reign. District horse races began in the reign of Queen Mary. In 1552 an annual horse race was established at Haddington and Lamington.

Why the slaughterman felt a bit sheepish

Until the middle of the nineteenth century the eve of Palm Sunday was observed as a holiday at the Grammar School in Lanark. The pupil who presented the master with the largest Candlemas offering was appointed king, and walked in procession with his life-guards and sergeants.

Bellman at Lanark.

Chambers, in *"Popular Rhymes of Scotland"* gives the following amusing account of Lanark in the olden time.

"It is reported that the burgh of Lanark was in former days so poor, that a single flesher, of the town, who also exercised the calling of a weaver, in order to employ his spare time, would never dream of killing a sheep until he had received orders for the entire animal beforehand. Ere commencing the work of slaughter he would call on the minister, the Provost, and the town council, and prevail upon them to take shares. But if no purchaser appeared for the fourth quarter, the sheep received a respite until such could be found. The bellman, or shallyman, as he is called there, used to parade the streets of Lanark shouting aloud the following advertisement:—

Bell·ell·ell
There's a fat sheep to kill!
A leg for the provost
And one for the priest.
The Baillies and Deacons
They'll take the neist;
And if the fourth leg we cannot sell
The sheep maun leeve and gae back
Tae the hill."

Ancient game of curling

The ancient game of curling was introduced by Flemish emigrants who settled in Scotland towards the close of the fifteenth century.

As St Andrews is the headquarters of golf, Edinburgh is the home of curling and in olden times city magistrates led a procession to Duddingston Loch for a game over the ice.

The game used to be particularly popular with women and in many towns and villages across Scotland it was customary for the married women to challenge the spinsters to an annual game.

The zeal and skill with which both parties pursued their pastime created much amusement amongst the bystanders.

An old rule book describes how to play the game: "The curlers range themselves into two opposing parties, and stand opposite to each other.

"They slide from one mark to another, large stones, of several pounds in weight, of a round form, and furnished with wooden handles. The aim of the player is, to lay his stone as close to the mark as possible, and in doing so, to strike away the best placed of his opponents.

"Each curler is provided with a broom, in order to sweep away the snow, or any other impediment from the ice."

Happy and unhappy feet

Folk at Forglen in Banffshire, along with residents of certain other Scots villages, regarded Friday as an unlucky day on which to be married.

The expressions, "happy and unhappy feet", were made use of by the inhabitants in the interchange of good and bad wishes. Thus, they wished a newly married couple "happy feet", and, as a guarantee against misfortunes of any kind, they saluted each other by kissing when they met on the road to and from church.

At Logierait, Perthshire, lucky and unlucky days were observed by many.

The particular day of the week on which May 14 happened to fall was considered to be unlucky throughout the remainder of the year.

Festival at Culross

St Serf was considered the tutelar saint of the ancient Fife village of Culross and an annual procession was held there in his honour on July 1.

Early in the morning all the inhabitants, from the youngest to the oldest, assembled and carried green branches through the community, decking the public places with flowers. The remainder of the day was devoted to festivity.

A boy and girl were King and Queen for a day at Candlemas.

Gifts for teacher
at Candlemas

Throughout Scotland on Candlemas Day it was customary for schoolchildren to make small presents of money to their teachers. The amount given depended on parents' means but sixpence (2½p) or a shilling (5p) were the most common sums. The boy and girl who gave most were respectively styled King and Queen.

The children were then given the rest of the day off and carried the King and Queen through their town or village, on a seat formed of crossed hands.

In some schools the teacher made a bowl of punch and this was dispensed, along with a biscuit, to pupils once the last sums of money had been handed over. They then all toasted the good health of the King and Queen.

The day concluded with a Candlemas blaze — either the burning of some wood in the neighbourhood or of an artificial bonfire.

An old popular custom in Scotland on Candlemas Day was to hold a football match — the east of the town against the west, the married men against the unmarried, or one parish against another.

Bell was placed in house of mourning at Hawick.

For whom the bell tolls

When a death occurred in Hawick one of the burgh officers walked solemnly through the town ringing his bell and issuing a general invitation to attend the funeral.

The bell was then taken to the house of mourning, and placed on the bed where the dead body lay. It was deemed sacrilegious to move it from there until the time appointed for the funeral.

*   *   *   *   *

A feature of every Highland funeral was *The Coronach* — these were songs generally in praise of the deceased, or a recital of the valiant deeds of his ancestors.

Rules of the travelling folk

The Society of Chapmen or itinerant merchants was a very ancient institution, given its original charter by King James V.

The annual general meeting of the Society was held alternately at Dunkeld and Coupar Angus. It was styled a Court and all members coming to the market were obliged to attend it.

They were summoned by one of the office-bearers, who, to enforce their attendance, went round the different booths and took a pledge in the form of goods or half a crown (12½p) in money.

Each member was obliged to produce his weights and measures, which were compared with standards, kept for the purpose. After the Court members dined together and spent the evening in some public competition of dexterity or skill.

Riding the Ring was a popular game on these occasions. Two perpendicular posts were erected, with a cross beam, from which a small ring was suspended. The competitors were on horseback, each bearing a pointed rod in his hand, and the one who passed between the posts at full gallop, carrying away the ring on his rod, gained the prize.

Into battle on
the Lammas morn

In the 18th century, during the early summer of each year, farmworkers in Midlothian formed themselves into bands — and each band erected a tower in a central locality to serve as a meeting place on Lammas.

The tower was built of sods; and was generally four feet in diameter at the base, and tapered towards the summit, which rose about eight feet from the ground. There was a hole in the centre for the insertion of a flagstaff.

Building started a month before Lammas — August 1 — and

during this period one of the band stood guard against attack from 'rival' communities.

In the run-up to Lammas each party appointed a captain. He was entrusted with the duty of bearing the standard which consisted of a towel borrowed from a farmer's wife, decorated with ribbons, and attached to a pole.

The standard was displayed on the summit of the tower early in the morning of August 1 and the assembled farmers waited, under the leadership of the captain, to resist an assault of the enemy.

Scouts were despatched at intervals to establish if any foes were near. At some engagements a hundred combatants would appear on each side. After a short struggle the stronger party yielded to the weaker; but there were occasions when things got out of hand and blood was spilled.

If no enemy appeared before the hour of noon, the garrison removed their standards and marched to the nearest village, where they ended the day's amusements with foot races and other games.

Drink this and live another year

Each year before sunrise on the first Sunday of May folk came from far and near to drink the waters of St Corbet's Well at the summit of the Touch Hills near Stirling.

By partaking copiously of the supply they were guaranteed to live for a further 12 months.

Husbands and wives, lovers with their sweethearts, young and old, crowded the hill tops in the vicinity of the well long before dawn, and each party on its arrival took lengthy draughts of the blessed water.

It is reported that St Corbet, after a lapse of years, deprived the well of its life-preserving qualities because of the introduction of "mountain dew" of a less innocent nature into these annual festivities.

The Maiden Feast

In parts of Perthshire a custom called the Maiden Feast marked the end of harvest. The last handful of corn reaped in the field

Maiden Feast in Perthshire

was called the Maiden. Matters were contrived to ensure that this fell into the hands of one of the prettiest girls in the field.

The special corn was then decked up with ribbons, and brought home in triumph to the sound of bagpipes and fiddles. A good dance was given for the reapers and the evening was devoted to merriment.

Afterwards the "Maiden" was dressed out, generally in the form of a cross, and hung up, with the date attached to it, in some conspicuous part of the house.

Drunkards shoot out at Dumfries

King James I was so delighted by the reception he received from townsfolk on a visit to Dumfries that he presented the burgh with the model of a small gun in silver.

Every seven years a shooting match was held and the winner was allowed to keep the gun until the next contest. The place of sport was a spot known as the King's Holm, about a mile below the town.

The competition became unpopular, however, because of a series of accidents blamed on drunken participants. As a local chronicler at the time put it: "It unfortunately happens that the important part of the festival, termed the 'Drinking' is never postponed as it ought to be, till the termination of the sport. The consequence is that the whole scene becomes one of riot and outrage.

"To show that people are not prevented from shooting when in a state of intoxication, a case is recorded of a man having once fired, when so overcome by liquor, that the gun was held for him by his friends, and yet he hit the mark, and was delclared victor, though it was said, he was not aware of his good fortune, nor conscious of the honours that were paid him till next morning."

John Mayne, in his Ballad of the Siller Gun sums it all up thus:—

"Louder grew the busy hum
Of friends rejoicing as they come,
Wi' double vis the drummers drum
The pint stoups clatter,
And bowls o' negus, milk, and rum
Flew round like water."

Drunken shoot-out at Dumfries.

Fairies stole their babies!

Odd though it may seem many folk in Invernesshire believed in fairies and their magical powers to as recent a period as the 18th century.

About 1730 in the village of Ardersier a man called Munro had a sick child which neighbours considered to be a changeling, substituted by elves at an unguarded moment, in place of his own.

A nearby hillock was famed as the scene of the moonlight revels of Titania and her court; and it was believed that if the

changeling was left there overnight, the real child would be found in its place in the morning.

The frightened dad actually put his child through this ordeal, and in the morning found it a corpse.

Meanwhile it was customary for fishermen in this village to marry at an early age. They didn't have the means to furnish a first home so the custom of thrigging was adopted by the young wife, a few days after marriage.

Accompanied by her bridesmaid she visited neighbours and friends who each presented her with some little household article.

Great fairs at Crieff

Much pomp and circumstance used to surround the opening of great fairs at Crieff by the Duke of Perth.

He held his courts, often in the open air, and afterwards rode through the market at the head of his guard.

He proclaimed his titles at the different marches or boundaries of his property.

Herring no more!

Church superstition at St Monans.

An ancient bell, suspended from a tree in St Monans Churchyard, Fife, and rung to summon people to worship, was removed during the herring season because fishermen believed in the superstition that its noise frightened the fish away.

Royal rulers

Today annual gala days are a popular highlight in the summer calendar, particularly in Lothian and Fife villages. A boy and girl are chosen as "Royal rulers" for the day. Every child gets a free picnic lunch and there are sports, competitions, and side-shows.

*Rolling out the barrel as a
young cooper ends his apprenticeship.*

A cooper's lot!

Many jobs have their own quaint customs.

On successfully ending their apprenticeships young coopers are covered in oil, feathers and sawdust by workmates and rolled in a barrel. But even this is threatened because there are fewer coopers around nowadays, as the beer trade uses metal containers instead of wooden ones.

Scramble story

Weddings are a day of great joy for the bride and groom and a time for mums and dads to shed a wee, but happy, tear.

For the kids however it means something quite different — the scramble or "poor oot."

These were first started centuries ago when it was the done thing for beggars, who assembled outside the wedding house, to be given leftovers from the feast.

'Poor Folks Purses' in the Royal Mile

Chambers, in "Traditions of Edinburgh" tells how beggars were given money at an annual ceremony in the Royal Mile.

"In that part of the High Street named the Luckenbooths, and directly opposite to the ancient prison house, stood two lands of old houses.

"Getting old and crazy the western tenement was entirely demolished, but the eastern portion was only refreshed with a new front of stonework.

"The remaining building was formerly the lodging of Adam Bothwell, Commendator of Holyrood House, who is remarkable for his having performed the marriage ceremony of Queen Mary and the hated Bothwell.

"At the back of this house, tradition states, Oliver Cromwell once had lodgings. He used to sit out and view his navy on the Forth.

"This building was called 'Poor Folks Purses' from this singular circumstance.

"It was formerly the custom for the privileged beggars known as 'Blue Gowns' to assemble in the Palace yard, when a small donation from the King was conferred on each of them.

"After receiving this dole they marched in procession up the High Street, till they came to this spot, when the magistrates gave each a leathern purse, and a small sum of money.

"The ceremony concluded by their proceeding to the High Church to hear a sermon from one of the King's chaplains."

So that is why they called it Boot Hill . . .

About seventy yards from the spot at Scone where Kings of Scotland were once crowned is a place vulgarly called Boot Hill.

Its other name is *Omnis Terra,* or every man's land.

Tradition states that at a Coronation folk came from all over with their boots covered in earth so that they might see the king "crowned on my own land."

Afterwards they cast the earth out of their boots upon this hill, hence the name Boot Hill or Omnis Terra.

Wild animal terror at spring of healing

Earlier in this book we told of various springs and their healing powers. One particular story is told in several Highland districts of Inverness-shire and Ross-shire.

In each case the spring rose in a circular hollow in a solid rock and the water was believed to possess the virtue of indicating whether a person would survive or not.

It was taken from the spring before sunrise and the patient was bathed or immersed in it. If the water appeared of a pure colour, it foretold recovery. But if it was a brown mossy colour then death was sure to follow.

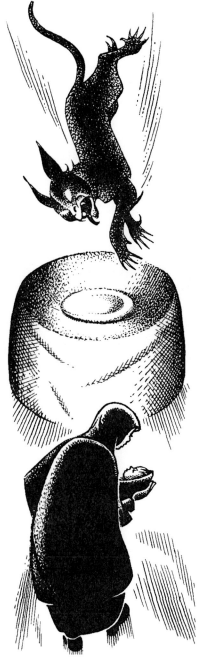

In the story of each spring an incident is related of a mother who brought her sickly child, a distance of between 30 and 80 miles, depending on location, to partake of the water.

But on approaching she was startled by the appearance of an animal, with glaring eye-balls, leaping into it. The poor mother considered this a fatal omen.

Her love, however, for her child overcame her fears. She dislodged the creature, and bathed her baby who afterwards slept much more soundly than before.

This seemed to confirm the healing virtues of the well, but in the case of the story told in Ross-shire, the child did not live long.

At around the same time two friends of a man who was not expected to live long, went to consult the same spring on his behalf and fetch some of the water.

On placing the pitcher in it, the water assumed a circular motion from south to west. They returned with joy, and told the patient that there was nothing to fear, as the motion of the water was a sure indication he would recover. Had it been from north to west he would have been doomed.

The man, needless to say, regained his health and went on to live a long and happy life.

Putting safely to sea on a goat and a prayer

Fishermen in the Western Isles used to hang a he-goat to the mast, hoping thereby to secure a favourable wind.

At the start of each voyage a special blessing was conducted. It opened by the steersman saying: "Let us bless our ship."
The crew replied: "God the Father bless her."
Steersman: "Let us bless our ship."
Answer: "Jesus Christ bless her."
Steersman: "Let us bless our ship."
Answer: "The Holy Ghost bless her."
Steersman: "What do you fear since God the Father is with you?"
Answer: "We do not fear anything."
Steersman: "What do you fear since God the Son is with you?"
Answer: "We do not fear anything."
Steersman: "What do you fear since God the Holy Ghost is with you?"
Answer: "We do not fear anything."
Steersman: "God the Father Almighty, for the love of Jesus Christ his son, by the comfort of the Holy Ghost, the one God, who marvellously brought the children of Israel through the Red Sea, and brought Jonah to land out of the whale's belly, and the Apostle St Paul, and his ship safely through the treacherous raging sea, and from the violence of a tempestuous storm, bless and conduct us peacably, calmly, and comfortably through the sea to our harbour, according to His Divine will, which we beg, saying, Our Father, etc."

Then, with the completion of the Lord's Prayer, it was deemed safe to put to sea.

Never a widower in the Western Isles

In some parts of the Western Isles, notably Barra, it was considered that a man who lost his wife should not remain a widower for long.

Indeed as soon as the funeral was over a tenant went to his laird and begged him to provide another wife who would manage the affairs of the croft.

The laird, such as MacNeil of Barra, wasted no time in providing the name and address of a new spouse and, armed with a bottle of whisky, the widower went to see her and arrange an immediate wedding!

When a tenant died his widow was looked after in a similar fashion.

Their family spirits

Almost every Highland and Lowland family, possessing any claims to distinction, had their own special demon or spirit.

One had the ghost of the hill; another the spectre of the bloody hand; and a third the little girl with the hairy left hand.

The little spectres called *Tarans,* or the souls of unbaptised infants, were often seen flitting among woods and secluded dells, lamenting in soft voices their hard fate.

The MacLean family had their headless horseman, who could be heard in the silence of the night careering on horseback round the castle ringing his bridle rein; the Ogilvies of Airdrie, fairy music; Kincardine Castle had its lady in green, who sat weeping beneath a particular tree when the dark shadow of death hovered near the family of Graham; the house of Forbes, their Lady Green Sleeves, and so on.

In Dumfries the county hangman went through the market every market day with a brass ladle or large spoon. He pushed this into the mouth of every sack of corn, meal, etc and carried it off full.

This was a traditional perk of office and the small quantity of produce taken out was called a 'lock' which explains why the hangman was often referred to as the 'lockman.'

But when the farmers refused any longer to comply with this old custom, the affair was brought before the courts which found in favour of the hangman. The response of the farmers was to boycott the market and for a long time they refused to sent their meal and corn there.

Burry man at 'Ferry and Handba' at Jed

Two of the most "painful" festivals held in Scotland today are the Burry at South Queensferry and the Handba' Game at Jedburgh.

At South Queensferry a local man dresses up each August in a long vest and is covered in sticky burrs from the Scots Burdock plant. Thus attired he visits each house in the town and those who make a donation are assured of good luck for the rest of the year.

The Jedburgh game is a free for all between the Uppies, born above the Mercat Cross, and the Doonies.

They battle over specially made cow-hide balls that are stuffed with hay. Wooden shutters are put over shop windows to save broken glass as the hours long battle rages through the town's streets.

There is one golden rule: the ball must not be kicked.

In the evening competitors retire to local hostelries for liberal supplies of ale to quench their thirsts.

Executions in olden times — the grim facts

It is a remarkable fact that the majority of "political" executions in Scotland,· even after the Reformation, were traceable directly or indirectly to religious controversy.

They date properly from the construction of the maiden by the Edinburgh magistrates in 1565.

It may be that the need of the maiden was brought home by the fact that the "auld heiding sword had failyet", and that the two-handed sword then bought from William Macartney was discovered to be too inconvenient and unserviceable.

Perhaps, too, so ingenious and consummate an instrument of death was deemed a fitting complement to the more complete judicial arrangements consequent on the erection of the Tolbooth a few years before.

Anyhow, this same maiden — with the occasional substitution of a new blade — continued to figure as the presiding genius or familiar spirit of the High Street and the Tolbooth for the next hundred ·and fifty years, the scene of her operations being generally the Cross, but occasionally the Castle Hill (she appeared in the Grassmarket only once or twice), while the west gable of the Tolbooth became more and more hideous with the grisly trophies of her prowess.

Those she caressed were not necessarily criminals of rank, nor even political criminals.

In Scotland the ancient custom of reserving the honour of death by decapitation for persons of birth and station had fallen somewhat into desuetude, though strangulation was still regarded as especially opprobrious.

Decapitation by the maiden seems, however, to have been chiefly confined to criminals under sentence from the judges of the supreme courts, and for offences of peculiar heinousness — as murder, rape, and treason.

None to whom this method of execution was deemed appropriate had been guilty of mere theft; and it must be remembered that while the maiden went on plying at the Cross, the hangman was also at work on the Borough Muir, and afterwards in the Grassmarket.

Among the more distinguished of the maiden's victims were the Regent Morton, the Marquis of Argyll, the Earl of Argyll, the Marquis of Huntly and the Earl of Gowrie — all executed at the Cross. Morton had been sentenced to the more shameful death of strangulation, but the sentence was modified by the king.

In two other conspicuous cases — those of the Great Marquis and Kirkcaldy of Grange — religious bigotry insured the substitution of strangulation for decapitation.

Both were executed at the Cross; but the method practised on the criminals at the Borough Muir was deemed the more fitting reward of persons excommunicated by the Kirk.

In Montrose's sentence it was specially mentioned that if at his death he was "penitent and relaxed from excommunication" the "trunk of his body" (his limbs were assigned conspicuous positions in the chief towns) was "to be interred by pioneers in the Greyfriars, otherwise to be interred in the Burrow Muir by the hangman's men under the gallows."

The fashion of Kirkcaldy's death was no doubt determined by what was held the necessity of fulfilling a prophecy of good John Knox — that he should "be brought down over the walls of it" (the Castle) "with shame, and hung against the sun"; and, as a fact, he was "put off the ladder" just after the sun, having passed the northwest corner of the steeple of St Giles, began to gleam down upon the scene.

It is a common error to suppose that Edinburgh has had but two chief places of execution, the Borough Muir and (later) the Grassmarket.

Even *Chambers' Encyclopaedia* compiled in this very High Street, within a stone's throw of these centres of history, will have it that "at Edinburgh the place of execution was chiefly in the Grassmarket till 1784, when it was transferred to a platform at the west end of the Tolbooth."

The only political executions of importance associated with the Grassmarket are those of certain leaders of the Covenanters — as Johnston of Warriston, Renwick, and others — all deemed only worthy of death by strangulation; but in the case of the Covenanters the extreme sentence was generally carried into execution immediately after capture, and in accordance with the regulations of martial law.

The Jacobite risings swelled in no inconsiderable degree the roll of Scots political victims; but the trials of the rebels-in-chief were held in London, and the Scotsmen who fell under the axe were made to follow in the footsteps of More and Cromwell and Strafford and Laud and — like the Greys, the Dudleys, and the Howards — they looked their last upon the world from Tower Hill.

Lockman puzzle of executioner's name

Lockman, Lokman, or Lockeman is the term that Scotsmen were wont to employ to designate the executioner.

Everywhere contempt and mockery rather than regard have been his portion; and that a people so accustomed to call a spade not only a spade but something worse should choose him an appellation so apparently colourless and inexpressive might fairly be termed a puzzle.

Yet the mild signification has been sanctioned — perhaps originated — by Sir Walter himself.

"Lockman", thus he has it, "so called from the small quantity of meal" (*Scottice*, "lock") "which he was entitled to take out of every boll exposed to market in the city.

"In Edinburgh the duty has been very long commuted; but

elsewhere the finisher of law still exercises, or did lately exercise, his privilege, the quantity taken being regulated by a small iron ladle which he uses in the measurement of his perquisite."

Now the facts on which Sir Walter's theory rests are indisputable; indeed, there is an abundance of evidence that throughout the Land o' Cakes the "lock" of meal was the hangman's perquisite from time at least anterior to the period when certain chalders of grain became the legal dues of the parish clergyman.

But this by no means settles the question how to explain that the hangman's collection of his salary in kind should be recognised even in his official description as his most distinctive function, all seeming allusion to his specific duties being omitted.

Superficially considered, the other derivation (originally sanctioned by Jamieson) from the better-known signification of the word "lock" as part of a door — the man who locks (*i.e.*, the "dubsman or turnkey") — appears more plausible; for no doubt the hangman and the gaoler were pretty often identical, the criminal being thus under charge of this grim representative of justice from the time that in the character of deempster (doomster) he pronounced the sentence of death against him, until his mortal remains were finally disposed of.

But again there is the difficulty — how to explain the seemingly almost morbid tenderness of the Scot's regard for the hangman's susceptibilities, in thus dropping all allusion to the more odious aspects of his office.

Be it remembered that the euphemism (if such it were) was accepted from time immemorial; so that you read in Blind Harry's "Wallace" that

"The Lokmen than thei bur Wallace, but baid
  On till a place his martyrdom to tak'."

Indeed, it is by no means improbable — so far as facts are known — that "lockman" was Scots for "executioner", when locks in Scotland were not specially associated with security, and sacks of grain in her market-places were scant and far between.

But what forbids the supposition that the epithet sets forth a grim allusion to locks of another kind?

Locks more distinctively associated with the doomsman's function? — the locks, to wit, of the man or woman whose finisher he was? — the locks by which he grasped the head to expose to the gaze of the gaping crowd?

Such a derivation, be it observed, is in no wise made superfluous by the fact that a "lock", or small handful, of grain, was the official perquisite; nor does it stand in contradiction to the custom, nor in the least diminish its significance.

On the contrary, it would explain (and this in striking accord with the sordid or brutal humour from which the Scottish vocabulary derives so much of its vigour) the origin and significance of the old word "lock" in Scotland as a quantative term. It was the quantity grasped by the executioner; that in any case, whatever else.

But let the derivation of the term be what it may, the custom referred to is proof enough that the lockman was very much in evidence.

A superficial observer might leap to the conclusion that his emoluments were out of all proportion to his duties.

Surely a handful of grain out of every boll in the market-place would mean more than a sufficient supply of food for himself and his family!

And had he not also a livery, a free house, and a special allowance for his more important appearances as well?

Plainly, therefore, for an official whose duties, albeit unenviable, were far from laborious (much less exhausting), such a salary would in frugal Scotland have been deemed inordinate.

But in those elder and sterner years the lockman did by no means loll away his hours in the listless fashion of his modern analogue. His life was busy as well as serious.

His diocese, it is true, instead of as now *(1893)* embracing three kingdoms, was contained within the bounds of a single burgh; but in olden time most burghs were able to keep their lockman in constant occupation, while in the larger towns he had to delegate some part of his duties to subordinates.

Strangled then beheaded

For one thing, the death sentence was attached to certain crimes now only dealt with by imprisonment (as theft and incest), or held deserving of no punishment at all — as adultery or attendance on the mass.

Again, the final ceremony was much more complex and more prolonged than now.

The criminal was not unaccustomed to address the crowd from the scaffold — occasionally he did so at great length; and when all was over, the body, in the case of strangulation, was commonly suspended for two or three hours before cutting down and decapitating, when it was customary for the hangman to continue his "watch and ward" on the scaffold till the performance of the final rites.

Hence the allusion of Dunbar in his "Flyting" —

"Ay loungand lyk ane lockman on ane ladder
Thy ghastly luke fleys* folkis that pass the by."

Nor did the lockman's responsibility cease with the public ceremony, for had he not to affix the several members of the more noted victims in conspicuous places, or sometimes to hang in chains the corpse of the heinous malefactor to dangle and rustle in the wind till it became a creaking skeleton?

And apart from his deathful duties he had plenty to do in the way of whipping, branding, and mutilation.

Not only was it his to apply the severer tortures in cases of exceptional guilt, whether actual or only suspected; he had also a well-nigh unbroken round of daily toil upon the persons of the less heinous.

* Terrifies

Many of these were handed over to him for punishment by the Kirk authorities; and the Session Records sufficiently indicate how much his services were in request.

Then he was under obligation to carry out the summary sentences of magistrates by bearing the culprit to the Cross and placing him in the jougs; the application of the pillory — with or without the delicate additions of pinching the nose, nailing the ears, or boring the tongue — usually communicated a spice of daily vivacity to the monotony of burgher life; the more momentous duty of ducking scolds and adulteresses occupied much of his solicitude; and to have omitted the observance of scourging criminals through the streets would have robbed market days of their primest flavour of felicity.

The "hangman's whip" had terrors more immediately effective than the "fear of hell", and perhaps it impressed the popular imagination more powerfully than either block or gallows.

In fact, it was chiefly in the lockman that both Church and State reposed their trust for the maintenance of order and morality.

None played so conspicuous a part in the public eye, and none discharged duties deemed more essential to the welfare of society.

His present effacement may indicate a marked improvement in morality, or a great advance in civilisation, or the discovery that many of his methods were really mistaken and ineffectual; but it is perhaps the most striking symptom of change to be recorded in the social and ecclesiastical life of Scotland during the last two hundred years.

Archery and golf?
Give us football!

The writer on football in an encyclopaedia affirms that, "unlike cricket, football had never taken root among the aristocracy and gentry."

This may be true of England from the time of Edward III's prohibition, but as regards Scotland it is altogether the reverse.

Each individual noble was a law unto himself, and the Scottish kings were by no means successful in substituting archery for football and golf.

Football was prohibited in 1424, 1451, 1471, and 1491; but the very repetition of the enactments is proof of their inefficiency.

At all events in 1497 footballs were purchased by James IV himself, probably for a game at Court.

In the next century the game was played not merely by the gentry, but even by the monks and other ecclesiastics.

Thus Sir Davids Lindsay's abbot vindicates his Presbyterial inefficiency by setting his prowess at football against his neglect of the pulpit:—

"I wot there is nocht ane among you all
More finelie can play at the fut-ball."

Even the highest nobles did not disdain the game. Of the "Bonnie Earl of Moray" the balladist sings:—

"He was a braw gallant
And he played at the ba';
And the bonnie Earl of Moray
Was the flower among them a'."

Another noble who "played at the ba'" was the fifth Earl of Huntly, who was seized with apoplexy (it was hereditary) while kicking off, and died the same night.

The game seems to have been a common one at the Court of Queen Mary.

Sir Francis Knollys tells that when she was at Carlisle after the flight from Langside, "about twenty of her retinue played at football for the space of two hours, very strongly, nimbly, and skilfully, without any foul play offered."

Their play struck Sir Francis as much superior to anything he had seen; and it is clear that the game in vogue at this time among the upper classes of Scotland differed radically from the common annual rough-and-tumble of later years.

True, James VI, in the "Basilikon Doron," published in 1599, denounces the pastime as "meeter for laming than making able the users thereof", but the modern forms of the game have been decried in similar terms.

The real cause of the decline and deterioration of football in Scotland was the prohibition of Sunday football by the Reformers.

The traveller William Lithgow, in his poem, "Scotland's Welcome to King Charles," 1633, laments that —

"Manly exercise is shrewdly gone,
Football and wrestling, throwing of the stone;
Jumping and breathing, practices of strength
Which taught them to endure hard things at length."

Beating home the harvest on Skye

Farmers on Skye had a curious way of showing their disapproval of neighbours who were slow to complete the harvest.

The one who finished reaping first sent a man or a maiden to the slowcoach with a bundle of corn.

He in turn sent a similar bundle to his neighbour, who was behind with his work, and so on until all the corn was cut down.

This offering was known as *"an gaolbir bhaeagh"*, but the person leaving it had to beat a hasty retreat. For, if caught, the farmer was entitled to give them a sound thrashing.

Whipped then expelled for playing the game

During the Covenanting and Cromwellian periods of ascendancy football was in still greater disrepute, and Sir David Hume of Crossrig records that, in 1659, having, in accordance with a traditional custom of the second-year students at Edinburgh University, taken part in a game of football on the Borough Muir on the 11th of March, he was sentenced to be whipped in the class, and, refusing to submit, was expelled the University.

Some have supposed that the ancient pastime in Scotland allowed running with the ball, as in the modern Rugby game, and in support of this Hone's account of the "historical game at Scone" has been quoted.

This game, however, as is stated in the original notice in Sinclair's "Statistical Account" of the parish, was only a carrying game, the use of the foot not being lawful; moreover, according to tradition, it was not of English origin, but was introduced into Scotland by an Italian in the days of chivalry; above all, it was notoriously peculiar to Scone, and hence the current proverb, "All is fair at the ball of Scone."

There is no evidence at all that carrying was permitted in the pure Scottish variety. Thus, in Skinner's "Monymusk Christmas Ba'ing" —

"Sometimes the ba' a yirdlins ran,
Sometimes in the air was fleeing";

but although the Monymuskers are represented as employing "a' the tricks of fut and hand", there is no allusion to any one running even a "yirdlins" with the ball in his arms, for that was only "fair" at Scone.

But is the Scone game not practically identical with the Greek and Roman with the *harpastum?*

Here, then, we seem to have a key to the origin of modern

Rugby. If at Scone, the presumption is that the Roman game was played in other parts of Britain; and Rugby football seems to be nothing more or less than a combination of the Saxon and Roman games, with a supplementary "scrum" derived from the period when football, having been under a ban in England from the time of Edward III, had degenerated into "a friendly kind of fighte", engaged in once a year by an unskilled mob, not infrequently in the narrow area of the public streets.

In all probability the ancient game of football in Scotland bore a close resemblance to the modern Association game, except that holding with the hand was allowed in certain emergencies.

It may have been quite as scientific, for constant practice at any game necessarily leads to the substitution of skill for mere brute force.

Skilled players would hardly care to take part in a game played with one hundred men or upwards a side, as in the border game of Sir Walter Scott's time, and we have seen that only about twenty players took part in the game before Queen Mary.

No doubt "accidents" at the game are still more numerous than is desirable, but the immense improvement — in the supercession of savagery by skill — which has followed the general adoption of the game by all classes of the community is undeniable.

Those who, by a long parade of "accidents", attempt to frown the pastime down as brutal and demoralising are merely doing their little best to make it both.

And, after all, is it as now played exceptionally dangerous?

Minor accidents are common enough; but, so far as loss of life is concerned, is football as perilous as hunting, shooting, riding, yachting, bathing, or even doing nothing?

Is it very much more deadly than crossing a crowded London street? or is it anything like so hazardous as railway travelling?

1893

In terror of the minister!

After the Reformation the Kirk of Scotland claimed the right to exercise absolute authority over conduct down to the minutest details.

While it abolished the confessional, it none the less aspired to regulate not merely the outward acts, but even the inmost sentiments and beliefs of every member of the community.

It assumed the entire moral charge of the nation individually and collectively; and the only possible means of escape from the rigours of its discipline was by the extreme expedient of committing a capital crime.

"Blasphemy, adultery, murder, perjury, and other crimes capital worthy of death ought not", says the First Book of Discipline, "properly to fall under censure of the Church", and this for the very sufficient reason that "all such open transgressors of God's laws ought to be taken away by the civil sword."

The Kirk had done with them, and therefore required of the State that they should be "taken away."

Every criminal — or rather sinner — who had not earned the right to be "taken away by the civil sword" was primarily answerable for his conduct to the Kirk authorities.

The crimes specifically mentioned in the Book of Discipline as "properly appertaining to the Church of God to punish the same as God's Word commanded" were "drunkenness, excess (be it in apparel, or be it in eating or drinking), fornication, oppression of the poor, by exaction, deceiving of them in selling or buying by wrong weight or measures, wanton words.

licentious living tending to slander."

The list is pretty comprehensive, but it is rather illustrative than exhaustive.

The Kirk had no complete and definite criminal code, as regards either specific acts or their punishment, the distinguishing characteristic of her criminal law being an extreme flexibility in the direction of inclusiveness and severity.

Practically any act, whether public or private, of any individual, whether gentle or simple, became a crime if the Kirk-session of his parish thought fit to make it so.

A similar flexibility also characterised her criminal procedure.

Mere suspicion was frequently sufficient to place a person under the ecclesiastical ban for years, if not even for life.

No strict laws of evidence were adhered to, but almost no method of obtaining evidence was too despicable to be rejected.

Spies in the Kirk!

Gradually the Kirk developed a system of espionage, which while much more harassing than the old confessional was quite as inquisitorial.

Every form of transgression, no matter how trivial, with every omission of religious duty, was searched out by elders and reported to the Kirk-sessions.

These "detectives" were told to attend fairs and races, and report on the conduct of those who frequented them; and, like the skeleton at the feast, their unbidden presence damped the spirits of the most jovial at every wedding and merrymaking.

None were permitted to claim exemption from surveillance.

"To discipline," decreed the inexorable Book, "must all the estates within this realm be subject if they offend, as well rulers as they that are ruled."

The Kirk's authority was deemed to be coextensive with the nation.

To plead non-membership of the Kirk, and decline attention on its ordinances, was simply to incur its implacable attentions; and should these prove ineffectual of repentance and submission, forth came the dread edict of excommunication.

The expelled person was delivered over to Satan, and declared to be "accursed", and "all that favour the Lord Jesus" were required so to "repute and hold him."

The effect of this was a system of "boycotting" so relentless that no choice was left but an unconditional surrender.

If the impenitent were a servant no master might employ him.

If he were a master no servant durst minister, on any pretence whatsoever, to his direst necessities; none might give him food, drink, or shelter; his nearest and dearest were debarred from offering him the offices of friendship or even showing him common courtesy; he became incapable of holding any form of property; his enemies might do with him as they liked without let or hindrance.

The absolute dread of excommunication

In Scotland excommunication was much more terrible than mere outlawry. Powerful nobles frequently defied the king with comparative impunity, but they could not so defy the Kirk.

Many examples illustrate this, but it may suffice to cite the cases of the first Marquis of Huntly, the ninth Earl of Errol, and the fifth Earl of Bothwell, all occurring during the reign of James VI, and at a time when the Kirk was by no means at the meridian of power.

Huntly, a Catholic by conviction, to escape the terrible results of excommunication, more than once came under solemn covenant to observe the ordinances of the Kirk and even to communicate.

Errol, less amenable to menace or persuasion, incurred in 1608 the penalty of £1,000 for absenting himself from communion; was enjoined to confine himself within the bounds of the city of Perth for "the better resolution of his doubts"; and being ultimately found "obstinate and obdured", was excommunicated, and laid in close durance in Dumbarton Castle.

As for Bothwell, being long the special champion of the Kirk, he was able with its countenance to defy the displeasure of King James, but having mortally offended the clergy he came under ban of excommunication, and had not only to put a final term to his alarums and excursions, but to depart the country and to spend the closing years of his life in penury and exile.

The secret of the Kirk's authority rested in her prerogative of excommunication; the curious blending of spiritual malediction with temporal tyranny in her anathema enabling her virtually to usurp the authority of the kingdom.

With such a tremendous weapon in reserve, too, she could afford to be comparatively lenient in her other modes of enforcing obedience; but the mildness of these subsidiary methods was more apparent than real.

Their seeming lenity was greatly qualified by comprehensiveness of application, and by the Kirk's persistent importunity.

Even attendance on religious ordinances was made to assume a disciplinary form, everything being excluded fitted to render the services attractive to the natural man.

While also regularity of attendance was imperative, wakefulness during services, however prolonged, was enforced by a variety of devices more ingenious than refined; and this was supplemented by periodical examination of every citizen, whether communicant or not, to test doctrinal soundness and progress in religious and theological acquirements.

No assumption of dullness or stupidity exempted from censure; for while great patience and forbearance were manifested towards weak-minded devotees, such persons as manifested any intelligence and ability in the daily duties of life were handled with the sternest severity if at all backward in the acquirement of that knowledge and those convictions essential to fit them to take their place as communicants.

"Everie maister of houshald", so it was decreed in the Book, "must be commandit eathir to instruct or ellis caus to be instructed his children servandis and familie in the principallis of the Christiane religioun. Such as be ignorant in the Articulis of thair Faith; understand not, nor can not rehearse the Commandimentis of God; knaw not how to pray; neathir whairinto thair richtuousnes consistis, aught not to be admitted to the Lordis Tabill.

"And gif thay stuburnlie continew, and suffer thair children and servandis to continew in wilfull ignorance, the discipline of the Churche must proceide against them unto excommunicatioun; and than must the mater be referred to the Civill Magistrat.

"For seing that the just levith be his awin faith, and that Christ Jesus justifieth be knawledge off himself, *insufferable we judge it that men shall be permitted to leve* and continew in ignorance as members of the Churche of God."

Thus the Kirk virtually menaced death against all who refused her yoke of intellectual and moral bondage.

It must also be remembered — though this may appear something of an anticlimax — that at stated intervals, as well as on special occasions, there were enjoined on all alike such fasts as did actually and literally occasion the severest qualms; and that this torture was ingeniously augmented by exposure to a prolonged series of exercises austerely diversified with exhortation and rebuke.

The system of public discipline introduced by the Kirk for actual transgression was to some extent a revival of an old Catholic custom which had fallen into disuetude; but it was characterised by the same bald and bare austerity that distinguished the Presbyterian ceremonials.

Whatever be said of certain modes of Catholic discipline there are few, if any, that verge on the ridiculous, while there are some (as that of pilgrimage) that are touched with a certain beauty and romance.

By her contempt for ceremonial, her dread of what she deemed to be idolatry, and her rejection of art, the Scottish Kirk necessarily deprived herself of a powerful means of kindling the imagination of her penitents.

Nearly all her modes of discipline were informed with a certain grotesque and awkward strain which tended to provoke the laughter of far other than the mere ribald.

Justice dispensed
on the "creepy chair"

The small delinquencies were commonly visited with admonition, and the formal admonition of adults in a public assembly is apt to seem more or less childish and pedantic.

But the chief disciplinary instrument was what Burns calls the "creepy chair."

There were two varieties — a high and a low; promotion to the more conspicuous depending upon the flagrance of the offence.

The professed penitent remained on the stool all through divine service, the presence of the congregation at worship being supposed to lend solemnity and severity to the chastisement.

Usually the offender was clad in a "harn gown" (the *San Benito* of the Presbyterian Inquisition), and various other signs of opprobrium might be attached at discretion.

Thus the discomfort of special offenders was further enhanced by the application of the branks — a vile contrivance in iron plates, whose chief function was to serve as a gag; and in the case of males the head was sometimes shaved.

For minor trespasses — as scolding, quarrelling, abstinence from church, violation of the Sabbath, playing at cards, and so forth — the usual punishment was confinement in the joug, an iron collar attached to the outer walls of the church.

This discipline was administered only on Sundays, but might be continued from week to week in succession.

A not uncommon alternative was fining.

Sometimes the defaulter was held in bondage for long periods in the kirk steeple; or the specially obdurate might be banished the parish, or delivered over to the magistrate to be scourged or burned on the cheek.

In extreme cases ducking in pools notoriously foul and rancid was also practised, some of the more enterprising Kirk-sessions equipping themselves with a special apparatus for the purpose.

During Knox's supremacy the ideal system of Kirk authority expounded in "The First Book of Discipline" was undoubtedly in full sway.

The principal memebrs of the nobility subscribed the book; the Privy Council of Scotland gave it their sanction previous to Mary's arrival from France; and although the Queen herself naturally declined to ratify it, the absence of her imprimatur rendered it no less operative.

It was not until the time of King James that the Kirk was shorn of much of her ascendancy, both in matters temporal and matters spiritual; but on one important point of discipline the harmony between Kirk and king was without jar or discord.

Both were equally exercised by and alarmed at the extraordinary manifestations of Satanic enterprise revealed in the presence of sorcery and witchcraft; James, because personally he greatly dreaded the application of witchcraft against himself; the Kirk, because it discerned in it a special attempt on the part of Satan to overthrow its own dominion.

Thus the chief result of the interest aroused in the community by the wonders recorded in the Jewish Scriptures, joined with the indefatigable attention the Kirk had seen fit to consecrate to the politics of the nether world, had been a sort of apotheosis of perhaps the most gruesome and repulsive of all superstitions.

Witchcraft superstitions

Of its astounding influence in depraving the popular imagination, the grave narrative of the Kirk historian, Calderwood, supplies a characteritsic example.

"In the monthes of November and December" *(1590)*, "manie witches were taikin: Richard Grahame, Johne Sibbet, *alias* Cunnninghame, Annie Sampsone, middewife, Jonet Duncan in Edinburgh, Eufame Macalzeane, daughter to umquhile Mr Thomas Makalzean, Barbara Naper, spous to Archibald Dowglas of Pergill, Jonet Drummond, a Hieland wife, Katherine Wallace.

"They conspired the overthrow of the king and queen's fleete, at their returne out of Denmarke, by raising of stormes upon the seas.

"Sindrie of the witches confessed they had sindrie times companie with the devill, at the kirk of Northberwick, where he appeared to them in the likenesse of a man with a redde cappe, and a rumpe at his taill, (and) made a harangue in manner of a sermoun to them; his text 'Manie goe to the mercat, but all buy not.'

"He found fault with sindrie that had not done their part in ill.

"Those that had been bussie in their craft, he said, were his beloved, and promised they sould want nothing they needed.

"Playing to them on a trump (Jew's harp), he said, 'Cummer goe yee before; cummer goe yee,' and so they daunced.

"When they had done, he caused everie one, to the number of threescore, kisse his buttocks.

"Johne Gordoun, *alias* called Graymeale, stood behind the doore, to eshew, yitt it behoved him also to kisse at last.

"John Feane, schoolemaister of Saltprestoun, confessed he was clerk to their assemblies."

Thus it would seem that the weird conventions of the wicked

were closely modelled after the assemblies of the Kirk down even to the preparation of an authoritative record of their desperate purposes and pactions.

The craze had indeed achieved a rankness of growth and a virulence of habit without parallel in the world's history; and the zeal displayed by the king in seconding the Kirk in her attempt to suppress the traffic with Satan and shield the prey of Satan's minions from calamity, went far to reconcile her to his lukewarm support in other fields of activity.

The breach between the Kirk and king did not become irreparable till the time of Charles I. The policy of Charles can scarce be defended, but it is at least as defensible as the policy of the Kirk.

His aims were not one whit more tyrannical than hers; intrinsically they were less so, for they had to do merely with "tithes of mint and anise and cumin", while she concerned herself with the "weightier matters of the law."

If the king endeavoured to interfere unduly with her forms and ceremonies, her persistent ambition was to subdue both king and people to her authority.

Thus she would have the covenant not only tolerated but subscribed by the king; and in the hey-day of her supremacy she endeavoured to impose it on England as well as Scotland.

In a sense her design was frustrated by Cromwell even in respect of Scotland, but although that great and masterful ruler debarred her from direct and active interference with the civil arm he permitted her while he reigned the exercise of almost unlimited control over manners and morals.

The session and the presbytery records, during the time of the Protectorate, teem with astounding instances of her interference with even the minutest details of domestic and social life.

A birch to
beat staff

Elders were appointed each in his own quarter for trying the manners of the people; and the Presbytery of Aberdeen went so far as to order every master of a house to provide himself with a "palmar", or birch, for the chastisement of frivolity in his family or among his maids.

But in 1690 this old form of discipline was knocked on the head by the repeal of "all Acts enjoining civil pains upon sentences of excommunication."

With this tremendous weapon all but innocuous in her grasp, the Kirk gradually discovered that her subsidiary methods of punishment were coming to be regarded with other than the old emotions.

The sanction of custom enabled her to retain them in position for some considerable time; but they had lost much of their impressiveness.

It was claimed that witchcraft did actually succumb to the vigilance of the Kirk-sessions, and when in 1743 further persecution of witches was forbidden by the civil authority, the Kirk protested against such enlightened legislation as "contrary to the express law of God; by which a holy God may be provoked to permit Satan to tempt and seduce others to the same wicked and dangerous snares."

But in truth witchcraft was chiefly a ghost of the Kirk's own raising, and the cruelties exercised in laying it form, perhaps, the darkest blot on her escutcheon.

It was the same with her efforts to cope with the vice of drunkenness, the increase in which may be partly explained by a desire to find a refuge from the gloomy dogmatism of the Kirk and the joyless social atmosphere of Puritanism.

As for the "cutty stool" as a moral influence: "A frail victim," says a church historian, "was sometimes compelled to appear on nine or ten successive Sundays exposed to the congregation in the seat of shame"; but "the most noticeable effect often produced by the exhibition was in the gibes and indecorous talk of the young peasants, who, after a few significant glances during the admonition, and a few words at the church door, adjourned the general question for discussion in the change-house."

In the later years of the nineteenth century the competition between the various denominations tended in the direction of moderation.

In any case, the more formidable paraphernalia of punishment nearly if not utterly disappeared.

The joug still hung by the outer wall of Duddingston Kirk — as a warning to the youth of adjacent Edinburgh against Sunday skating on the neighbouring loch perhaps.

The stool of repentance also ceased to vary the monotony of Presbyterian ceremonial and — a Samson shorn and captive — could be contemplated without alarm in antiquarian museums.

After years of degenerate and spurious observance, the Fast Day was avowedly consecrated to recreation and frivolity.

As to the services, even in those sections of the Kirk which specially claimed to represent "the distinctive principles of the Reformation", it was now recognised that the proper means of ecclesiastical influence was not compulsion and mortification but persuasion and charm.